A Summer Home

by Tom Sato
illustrated by Robin Kerr

Core Decodable 111

McGraw Hill Education

Bothell, WA • Chicago, IL • Columbus, OH • New York, NY

MHEonline.com

Send all inquiries to:
McGraw-Hill Education
8787 Orion Place
Columbus, OH 43240

ISBN: 978-0-02-145841-7
MHID: 0-02-145841-3

Printed in Canada.

9 10 11 12 KOD 24

Last summer, Dad was thrilled. He had a large new awning! It was green and white. It could shade the backyard porch.

It was not hard to open the awning. Dad just hit a button. A little motor turned on, and the awning rolled out.

Early one day, I was on the porch. The awning was rolled up. I heard a bird. I looked up.

A bird was perched on the rolled-up awning. It had started to make a nest there. I called Dad.

The bird flew away. In a hurry, Dad grabbed a short ladder. He climbed up it. He looked at the nest.

"So far, this is just twigs," Dad said. He brushed them away.

"The bird will learn not to make a nest here."

I was surprised. Dad could tell.

"Do not be concerned," he said. "This will not hurt the bird. It will learn."

At first, the bird did not learn. Each day it perched on the awning. Each day, it started to make a nest.

Each day, Dad brushed the twigs away. After the third day, the bird stopped. It must have made a nest far away.

"See," said Dad. "The bird is smart. It searched for a better place."

The next Sunday we visited a farm.

On Thursday, we came back. On the porch, Dad heard a bird. He grabbed his ladder.

"A nest with eggs!" he whispered.

I was concerned. Would Dad brush the nest away? He did not.

"Now this nest is a home," he said.

All summer, Dad did not start the motor.
And he did not open the awning.
New birds were born and grew.

Later in the summer, Dad placed tin over the rolled-up awning. Birds cannot make a nest there. We can use the awning.

Dad learned!